THE FULCRUM

THE FULCRUM

SELECTED POEMS 2000-2010

SAM ROGERS

GOWEN PLACE PRESS

BAINBRIDGE ISLAND, WASHINGTON

ISBN: 978-0-9847183-0-6

10 9 8 7 6 5 4 3 2 1

Gowen Place Press
Bainbridge Island, WA 98110
gowenplacepress@yahoo.com

Cover photo by Ken Turner

Contents

SECTION 1: THE LIGHT

Nocturnal

I've been graced beyond measure,
I realize, sitting up late at night,
reflection dark in the window,
but lose the joy incessantly,
within moments
of arrival,
departure.

Sudden debate
among geese in the harbor.
Inside, furnace clears its throat,
breath of sleeping bodies stirs the air,
as the great flood of being engulfs
both center and circumference,
flinging itself recklessly,
into Douglas fir and woodpiles,
sea otters and water rats,
into the fatigue behind my eyes,
the clumsiness of fingers,
the separation I can't quite span
to reach the desired bliss.
Yet even this frustration
holds the ridiculous truth:
that what I want is as close
as I am to myself.

Closer.

Technique

Technique?
Some potion or position?
Some knack to pick up
like riding a bicycle?
Meditation regimen?
A certain aroma?
Daily communion?
A rosary in the hands?
A scapular, remember them?
(brown cords across the shoulders
attached to rectangular emblems
of Mary on my chest,
the Sacred Heart of Jesus
on my back)
A piece of the true cross?
Bone from a saint?
The Buddha's eyelash?

Deckhand mops the floor.
Engine vibrates my sternum.
Reading glasses are smudged,
So I clean them.

Spellbound

And to die is different from what any one supposed,
and luckier.
Walt Whitman

Incandescent yet completely full,
death is masked by the tombstone illusion:
a magician with dandruff on the shoulders
of his greasy tux appears to disappear us
in puffs of corruption.

Yet what if this dreaded end
is only a beginning?
Recall the most intense pleasures
of your life and fill in the blanks.
With these, let us say, the wonders
of death will have only begun,
transcendent amends
for lives of both quiet
and noisy desperation.

Of course, this forbidden
apple of knowledge
would be mercifully withheld
lest we be lured, with the lemmings,
to sprint, over the cliff, into the sea.

Because even ecstasy has limits:
arriving in heaven, Captain Stormfield found
mounds of harps and haloes discarded in the clouds
by the eternally bored. Caught in the brilliance
of endless bliss, we may be tempted again
to summon the darkness,
live in a body, look out through its eyes,

feel the suspense inherent
in confinement to a self,
and end up just as we are right now:
rabbits who are always
being launched from a hat.

The Hound Of Earth

I fled Him down the labyrinthine ways of my own mind...
from The Hound Of Heaven by Francis Thompson

He looked in the china closet
and in the commode.
He went through boxes in the garage
he hadn't opened since college.
He looked on the Roman Wall of Mt. Baker,
the surface of ice up close to his nose.
Everywhere, he found
arrangements of molecules,
some mundane or irritating,
others vivid and seductive,
but not what he wanted.
He searched in books, in movies,
in Protestant and Catholic churches,
in Buddhist temples. He bought items
at the mall and looked in the packages.
He delved into bottles of beer and wine.
He ran thousands of miles. Out in the garage,
he lifted tons of weight. He attended school
and went to work. He rummaged
through his thoughts, meditated
on their emptiness, fell
in and out of love,
unbuttoned blouses, unzipped skirts,
liked what he found,
but didn't find what he sought.

One afternoon in May,
he stopped looking.
Outside, sparrows argued at the feeder.
The cat came in, rubbed her face
against his shoe.
Light hovered by the chair.

Pater Noster

At the wedding of tide and moon,
water is turned to mud.
The head of Eagle Harbor swings a censer,
fragrance of holy ooze
from whence our forefathers
once slithered. I walk the path
with Joe and Matt, beset
by thickets who art
within the headland's
spongy hummocks.

Beneath Jupiter's solemn gaze,
we stand on margin of quagmire
and cast stale loaves,
but no birds appear.
In the flood of dusk,
gulls, geese, ducks, and terns
have all missed mass.
Even the synod of crows
has recessed.

Our daily bread languishes
uneaten, on tussock as it is in mire.
We retreat to the wildwood,
trespassers whose temptations
have already been delivered.

The rising moon is held
in a sieve of boughs.
Light leaks through
to flow upon our faces.
Creatures shift in tangle of brush
as we talk of how the world is born

from the emptiness behind our eyes,
emptiness as alive as the spider
rappelling from fern tip to trillium.

Hallowed be the emptiness,
its kingdom come to hold us,
on the water as it is in woods,
in the night as it is in stars,
in my sons' hands
as they are in mine.

How To Get Lost

Step 1: Jump into a body.

In a ground floor apartment in Morton, Pennsylvania,
across the street from the Boeing Vertol plant,
listen to John Coltrane play "My Favorite Things"
and mime the fingerings even though
you can't play the sax.

Sit at edge of mesa,
boots dangling in the drop,
skimmed by hasty sparrows,
and stare at Chimney Rock.

In a Manhattan apartment so hot that clouds are forming,
watch "The Shop Around The Corner," directed
by Ernst Lubitsch, script by Samson Raphaelson,
and find yourself absorbed by a store in Budapest
during the depression. Fall in love
with Margaret Sullivan.

Hungover on New Year's Day, run fast
in Riverside Park, keeping pace with ice floes
gliding down the Hudson.

Take the White River Trail to Thunder Creek,
try to force your way to the basin above,
grapple with devil's club along the ravine,
ending up suspended by thorned vines
above the turbid water.

At the Compline service
in St. Mark's Cathedral,
follow the voices
ascending in the vault.

Leave your icy tent at midnight,
climb all night to summit of Rainier,
as sun rising from plains to East
suffuses air in gold.

Step 2: Die.

Get born, die, get born.
Repeat as needed,
until done.

Mass In B Minor

Racing from night shift down to the ferry,
through the encampments under the viaduct,
in the narrow gate where the host disembarks,
overseen by the eye behind dawn's eye,
I stumble on patched asphalt of ramp suspended
above the greased sheen that heaves at pilings,
laps at the bulkheads, as gulls hurtle past
below clouds massing in
to confront the Cascades.

Under Magnolia's bluff, thousands of masts,
yet no one under sail, as Odysseus snores at home
or chisels frost from the window of his Lexus.
While the city bares its broken teeth,
our boat, set free, drifts off from the dock,
shoved by the wind, across the chop,
until we surge into whitecaps
pursued by the gulls
who play in our wake.

As I pant and sweat on bench of vinyl,
I receive the offering of the day:
a cough, a laugh, a flush, a rumble,
crinkle of wrapping, taste of fruit leather,
rattle of news stands, incense of brine
that flows in cold through open doors,
until I walk forward
and flip the switch
to seal them.

Past broken pilings of Luna Park,
bearing spirits on coasters and ferris wheels,
the power of clear light brings Alki Beach

into communion, zooms in on a man
who leans on the railing of his balcony,
curiously lucid below the clouds.
In this glow, we're being created,
down to the rust bolts,
and grimy tiled floors.

Sleepy people venture out to the bow
and then retreat with cries of "Cold!"
Pressure in my shoulder, flash of a camera,
man in a suit peruses pamphlets on the rack,
blower clicks off, warning tape flaps,
scraping of seats, grind of a dustbin.
In the aisle, a little girl dances,
hands poised above her
like heads of geese.

Over the island, mountains, veiled
by snow, shed low clouds that blend
into this breadth of water, silver-gray,
crossed with endless undulations,
patterns laid on textures upon patterns,
clear, elegant, and precise,
in contrast to this mind:
foggy, imprecise, and rather crude,
yet redeemed by what is.

Children discuss goldfish and whales,
surface of green deep cracks into white
at the crests of waves. We turn to avoid
the curving sand that bars the harbor.
Tugboat pulls a barge, fog hangs in shreds
in trees of Wing Point, bird dives down
but then doesn't emerge,

flying below us
on winds of water.

Engines cut, we glide toward the yard
where ancient ferries gather. Waves surge by,
shadow of our boat slides on the pilings,
gulls hover at the windows, eyeing our eyes.
Scull slips past, oars dip and rise
in blessing, until bow butts dock,
and we are held, in time,
as the chalice holds the wine,
as the body holds the blood.

Orison

Bring a smooth stone
that I might heft,
the weight of it
sleeping in my hand.

Bring me such a stone
and I will pledge my fealty
although your face
is always turned away.

That stone I shall carry
through ruptures and joinings
until its circled shadow
is worn into my palm.

Then when you are through,
lead me to the field of stones
where I'll lay it down in rain
upon what had to be.

If this gift should please
your grace, alter me
back to bone, one
with stone, at last.

SECTION 2: THE DARK

The Prince Of Darkness

Brings a tainted casserole
to the neighborhood potluck,
fiddles incessantly with the wiring,
sets out bowls of anti-freeze
for trespassing pets, pours
extra cheese on the saltiest chips,
trades crack and crystal for blowjobs,
greases the rungs
of the pre-school monkey bars,
pores over maps, cigar in hand,
planning bloody yet pointless invasions,
carries razors, pills, and a loaded Glock 9
for the convenience of the depressed,
skulks in the blood cells,
thumb on the stem
of his bitter stopwatch,
pays God under the table
for franchise rights.

When we cry our dismay,
the Prince smirks and confides:
without the serpent, no history.
Without Judas, no Easter.
And without death,

(wait for it now,
the big finish)

nothing matters.

In Stygian Condo

I didn't really want to die
but by the time my heart stopped
I was ready for a change.

How was the pain?
On a scale of 1 to 10, it was a Q,
maybe an ampersand.

My dead relatives insist
that I will soon get used to this
but I wish I had a manual.

I hear rumors of a meeting
I'm supposed to attend
but don't know where or when.

What I miss most: sunsets,
books, popcorn, and the World's
Wildest Police Chases.

Everyone is friendly enough
but I find that it's really hard
to get to know people.

My former pets follow me around:
three dogs, seven cats, and a hamster
I'd completely forgotten.

I'd like to get some exercise
but in every direction,
a lack of resistance.

Apparently, none of my exes
has yet arrived. At least
that should be interesting.

A place like any other,
except for a noticeable
absence of features,

where I have the feeling
that something is always
just about to happen.

The Big Desire

In the empty movie palace,
    the lights are about to dim.
        Is this the moment? Now?

His Lover hides upon this earth.
    He stalks Her in every bar
        and suspects Her in every face.

After a day of driving drunk
    through the smoke of burning fields,
        he drops his engine on the Interstate.

In a motel room whose locks are broken,
    roaches dance their writing on the wall.
        He bares his neck and prays for Her incisors.

Ida Lupino ripples in his tears
    as she glides forward into focus
        to wait for Robert Mitchum's kiss.

A thousand yards away, on the moon-smacked ridge,
    his Lover snaps the sacred bolt,
        adjusts the cross-hairs on Her sight.

The film jumps, catches in the gate.
    Their final clinch is suspended, melts,
        and crackles brown to light.

Yi-Han The Younger

Emperor Yi-Han the Elder
was not a beloved ruler, yet
his warfare was tempered by reason.
He drove away marauding vandals
but held his vengeance at their border.

Yi-Han the Younger had no such wisdom.
He fancied himself a swordsman
because experts deftly let him win.
Mindful of his many executions,
retainers assured him that he was kind.

In the heat of summer, vandals
pierced the wall, impaled the heads
of innocents agape on stakes,
burned two cities. The vandals
themselves died in the flames.

From dreams of burning palaces,
Yi-Han the Younger awoke in sweat,
startled his wife, said the gods wanted war.
The Imperial Council ratified his edict
and shook each others' hands.

With ponderous haste, the imperial army
pulled wagons through the breach.
Uncertain of the enemy, they killed
all who resisted, declaring afterward
that they must have been vandals.

Troops then advanced through the desert.
Villages burned, wells were poisoned.
Supply lines stretched across the sands

as caravans returned, laden with plunder.
Ravens grew fat on the corpses.

At autumn equinox, peasants thronged
to buy the harvest at the markets.
Children of vandals mingled easily.
Under their cloaks, bags of black powder
ignited into pink clouds of flesh.

Winter solstice, at the Temple of Heaven,
Yi-Han and his wife made sacrifice.
In the entrails of pigeons, examined
by obsequious priests, Yi-Han found
divine approval for his course.

Yi-Han decreed at New Year, his eyes
snow blind, that vandals were everywhere
so war would have no end. The peasants
bowed their heads and muttered,
"We've all been cursed by the fear
and greed of Yi-Han the Younger."

Good Night

"Eighteen straight whiskies. I think that's the record."
Dylan Thomas' last words

A man wore his backpack
while sitting on the railing.

When the ferry turned
into the mouth of Eagle Harbor,

the weight of the pack
pulled him back.

He fell in the water
and has yet to arise.

A young woman called the Crisis Line,
said she was suicidal, but agreed

to the appointment I offered.
Later that day, she escaped

from her family, and drove
north, to Deception Pass,

where she jumped from a cliff,
her blouse flapping up

to cover her face
before she hit the water.

On a May evening in 1968,
my father strolled along a dock

outside a restaurant on the Delaware
River. He smoked a cigarette

then walked the plank
to a cocktail lounge on a schooner.

His knee, shattered in '48
when he bailed into the Gulf

from a burning plane, locked up.
He stumbled, hit his head,

and slid into the water. They all
found their way by plunging

into that good night
and, after the rage and fear

dissolved, were finally taken,
gently, in the water's ebbing light.

Awake, on the Sound,
on the Earth, or in dreams,

I sail over their bones.

Possum's Not Playing

Head snapped to the right
in blur of street sky
red black
done.

As family undertaker of fauna,
I was assigned to dispose of the body,
splayed just beyond the left front tire
of our parked Impala.

The deceased was one
of America's only marsupials,
who lurk like ghostly rats,
and defend themselves
by playing dead
and tasting bad.

But this was no act:
sharp head squashed flat
in pool of lampblack,
blood filling eye socket,
trickling from ears.
Gums were exposed
above a snarl of teeth.
Gray fur jutted out
in macabre wet spikes.
The naked tail emerged,
worm-like, in loops
from under the body,
torn to reveal
glistening bulge
of intestine.

Even at its best, who could
love such a creature?
Averting eyes, bating breath,
I scraped up the corpse
with a flat black shovel,
metal grinding on pavement,
leaving behind
driblets of meat.

I carried it at arm's length,
in a hefty bag, to a can in the alley,
where it dropped with a thud.
I clamped the lid tight
to impede scavengers
and joined my family
to eat a turkey.

Next morning, a cry in the yard:
another possum wandered
erratically, searched
in the shaggy grass,
under the rhododendrons,
around the green sand box
with the head of a turtle,
keening for its mate.

On War

In the aftermath of suburban cataclysm,
amid the tread marks of mad bulldozers,
the tree declined at an angle to the planet,
like a missile flung by the Russians,
corona jammed in dirt, roots uplifted
to light in a writhing tangle taller than me.
The trunk, scarred with fissures, lay beside
an open trench that held rain and bred mosquitoes.
Weeds and grass webbed the sandy soil that was filled
with soggy cardboard, nails coated in tetanus,
and shards of glass, glinting in the sun,
eager to slash the thin soles of Keds.
Our back yard, more dandelions than grass,
blended easily into this feral terrain
between split-levels and highway,
where my brother Joe and I escaped
from even younger brothers in laden diapers.

Dad smoked one continuous Lucky Strike,
lighting his next from the butt in hand,
an eternal torch ignited in Navy flight school
where they'd handed out coffin nails for free.
The smoke spewed out of him in plumes
that permeated clothes and leathered skin,
rendering his breath as sulfurous as a volcano's.
Always wary he would blow,
Joe and I envied his easy command of hell.
As the stereo played Night On Bald Mountain
and he drank whiskey neat,
I'd fumble through his jacket pockets,
snatch cigarettes and matches,
so I too could be the master of fire.

Down the weeks of summer,
Joe and I played army, slick
with sweat, embossed with bug bites,
crawling on elbows and bellies
under shrapnel and barbed wire,
wielding machine guns from Woolworth's,
to guarantee the freedom of the fallen tree.
When the Air Force jets cracked sonic booms,
we waved at their fleeing shadows,
imagined Red Army tanks exploding
like fireworks on the 4th.

A sizzling day, but Joe had an earache.
Alone by the trunk, I stewed in its shade,
the heat bearing down on me
like a North Korean interrogator.
I lit matches and tried to ignite the bark
but the damp wood kept snuffing them out.
I used the last one to set the matchbook ablaze
so the words: *Admiral Restaurant and Lounge*
were crisped in brown and consumed
by orange embers. I jammed
the smoking remains in a knothole,
and walked back home to watch
a combat movie on The Early Show.

That night, in our bedroom, air swollen and acrid,
as a baby cried somewhere in exhausted gasps,
I thrashed on the bottom bunk in the tangle
of bucking bronco sheets, kicking the slats
above to torture Joe, only stopping
when he threatened to tell.
The Funeral March Of a Marionette
drifted in from the blue flicker
of Alfred Hitchcock Presents.

I coughed from smoke
as sleep dipped, swirled,
and finally fell.

A siren, closer than usual:
staccato flickers of primary colors
danced in the mirror, pulsed on the bureau,
splayed across the ceiling. I lurched
to the window and looked through the screen
at our tree become ecstatic:
blazing banners flapped from its sides,
coals glowing in the seams
launched missiles of flame
that burst in smoky clouds.
A fire truck, its bulk cut
from black by hazard lights,
left the highway to cross the split land,
its headlamps bouncing wildly,
alternately pinning me in glare,
releasing me to night.

Homeopathic

When my son saw me
light up on a summer's eve,
he cried, "Dad, you're going to die!"

Now, I sit with a cigar
in the rain, barely kept dry
by the overhang.

I don't inhale but can feel
how smoke works its way
into the soft meat of my jaw.

My dad smoked Lucky Strikes
and couldn't ever quit
but died in water, not by fire.

Water surrounds me now,
falls fast, drips
through snarl of branches.

I draw in the smoke,
watch the rim of embers
grin beneath the ash.

Are you in this moist air?
The woods reply with silence
as nicotine surges in my blood.

If I move my hand
a few inches to the left,
drops sizzle on the coals.

I will finish this cigar.
I will put down these words.
I will go to sleep.

Still, waiting for the ash
to fall, your son sits
smoking in the rain.

Quite Contrary

The boy with x-ray eyes peered
through your Catholic school uniform:
dark wool jumper, knee length,
light blue blouse with Peter Pan collar,
black and white saddle shoes.
We circled each other at the science fair,
until you sidled up to my geologic chart;
eras that separate us now.

Duplex in Havertown, false brick siding,
your father at the kitchen table, head in hands,
aftermath of his weekend binge.
Your mother, Irish and garrulous,
talking more to me than you did
while I pretended to be nice
but thought only of your body.

You were trained by the Legion of Mary
in the avoidance of advances,
trained by your brothers in the shoulder bump,
the slap, hip check, and tickle,
but most of all you were skilled at teasing me
for my clumsiness, my gravity, my stiff devotion.

Driving down Baltimore Pike
in my black Ford Fairlane
when the hood flew up, blotting out the world.
We careened to the shoulder, panting
with laughter, used the strap
from your purse to tie it down.

Tongues tangled in dentition,
inside someone else
for the first time since birth,
grinding the gears of time
in the front seat of the car.

My parents out of town, event as rare as a comet,
down in the basement beside the bumper pool table,
I removed your blouse, breasts pale and cool,
until your sadness deflated desire
and I buttoned you up.

Mornings in the car in the vast gravel lot,
students laughing at the clouded windows,
my fingers stealing under edge of elastic:
wiry hair, jungled, terrain of desire;
you didn't move, barely breathed,
your face turned away. Through the day,
I'd breathe you
in from my hand.

Beside my callow poems,
your drawing for the magazine,
schooner tilted in the wind,
sails at full term, bursting from the frame.

After graduation, I tried
to ignore the obvious:
when you broke up with me,
in the car, of course,
the steering wheel carved
a bow in my forehead.

Half a year later, you came to me at college,
lay down on the bed in my narrow dorm room,
closing your eyes. A knock on the door,
I rose up to answer, let in my new girlfriend,
and you were gone, once again.

You dropped out of art school,
pregnant and married, but not by me.
Five years later, at a party,
tremulous, I sat beside you,
our spouses on either side.
The music was loud and I was drunk,
so leaned over and whispered,
"You know I still love you."
So close that I inhaled your breath,
you looked me in the eye, and said:
"I can't imagine why."

Astray

My hands are numb,
my face is scratched.
Should I stay by a tree?
I pat the nearest, a pine
or Douglas fir, I guess,
and wonder if, instead,
I should follow the stream
down the brush-choked ravine,
below the red of infected sky
to find a lake surrounded
by the solace of cabins?
I'm tired and have no food.
I'm wearing jeans and a cotton shirt,
soaked through with sweat.
Night is rising, cold is rising,
from mists in the ground.
I last saw other hikers
three hours ago
but my shouts were absorbed
by the forest mass.
I hear the flutter of wings
above me. Those lights,
I hope they're stars.
I don't know
if it's early or late.
I can't wander
any longer
so push together a heap
of pine needles, branches,
dirt and moss,
and crawl inside,
to wait.

The Waning

Drunk and stumbling, singing carols off-key
to keep shadows at bay, home from college

on Christmas Eve, I leaned close to a candle,
near the wobble of flame, and blew:

wax flew in my eye, pain that lasted for weeks
until a scrap of it slipped from my cornea,

floated out on a tear. Now, decades later,
when I look at the flat gray of a glowing sky,

and lose focus, I see, floating across my vision,
the scar left by that wax, a scrawled line

with looping tail and bowed head, the mark
of the beast who eats my years.

The Situation

This is a slow burn,
with each of us a fagot
on our very own pyre,
sun lost in the smolder
from a mountain of tires.

Scorched bear coughs, rolls
into a creek. Out of the blaze
stumble marmots and fox.
Copters dump their buckets
but only splash the rocks.

No more self-deception,
this is the frying pan:
the eggs begin to smoke,
flames gnaw the cook
who laughs and jabs the yolk.

SECTION 3: THE FULCRUM

On The Fulcrum

a wedding poem

The air we fall through in the plummet
is the air we gulp on rising from the deep.
The earth that fills our graves
is the earth that grows our wheat.
The water that engulfs us
is the water that slakes our thirst.
The fire that consumes us
is the fire that melts the ice-bound heart.

In the turning of contraries,
all things will come to us,
together and apart.

For the chain that binds us to the rock
could be the chain that lifts the anchor
so we can set sail
out of the ancient harbor
out to the open sea.

Break

She bucks hay all morning
in the barn until
her head bumps the ceiling
and her shirt sticks to her skin.
The air is a fog of straw
that scrapes her eyes and throat,
clings to her tied-back hair.
She jumps from the stack,
tumbles in the chaff,
and runs outside to stagger
blind in the sun.

Over in the willows,
back again to the well,
she drops the bucket
down the mossy dark,
the rope hissing
in her callused hands.
The splash sends a breath
of cold up to her face.
She stirs the depth
then cranks, weight
rising to the creak
of the wooden pulley.
She ties off the rope,
hugs the circle
of dripping slats,
puts the bucket to her lips
and leans back.

The torrent falls,
numbing her head
and cloaking her in silver,
as she drinks deep
from the splintered brim.

Sunday At The Fair

Twisting sheets of sleet
followed by spangled blue,
bands of storm clap hard,
bring sudden windswept clarity.
At dusk, tree cracks, high wire
sparks, lamps surge, then die,
video images are tapped
by a wand and disappear
so the boys read
and I scribble while the cat
with conjunctivitis,
sore eye glaring,
sneezes on the couch.
If this were a fairground,
the rides would be closing,
the carnies headed off
to their trailers seeking
liquid oblivion.

Light from the last sun
flares through the curtains,
expires as the next skirt of cloud
shimmies through,
the world determined to flaunt
its essential volatility,
a given for me but hard to anticipate
for the boys, who have tickets
for thrills and terrors all their own.
Our pages flick by, words
darting to red balloons
that will pop to reveal The End.
Night rubs off the greasepaint
to reveal the shadows of its face.

In our room, the Midway is quiet
except for the tumble
of cotton candy cones.

Out of a dead composure,
with the crank of gears,
screech of rusty pipe,
a carousel stirs into action.
The cat yowls and flees,
the boys sit up on the couch,
hoping to be amused.
With a flash of revolving mirrors,
a unicorn slides up its pole,
and Calliope plays her music,
as the power returns.

Spinneret

Single strands of spider web
brush against my skin as I walk
in the dark to the ferry.

The spiders in the brush grunt
with disappointment when I proceed,
their biggest prey so easily escaping.

I admire their optimism
as they launch these merest of threads
out on the currents of air.

The floating strands could be
a language, articulated
from the depths of their viscera.

They send out these lines of silk
like poems, hoping with a subtle graze
to intercept the flight of their game.

And when a reader is arrested,
they'll slip down the filaments to inject
the insidious protein of words.

In Thrall of Nox

I live between moon's rise and slash of dawn
and taste the fizz of stars upon my tongue.
The dark-drunk Queen bestows on me a kiss
to bid me come and share her bawdy jests.
I climb inside her dimly damasked coach
above the web of glints and sparks below.
We skim the flesh of clouds to rouse the rain
that spills upon the bellies of the fields
where loam soaks up the flow of liquid grace.
But when an eastern ember flares, then glares,
Nox flies to west and leaves me to Sol's wrath.
Disdaining now to spare the mind of night,
with waking force, day blasts the secret paths
and burns my vision dry in ruthless light.

Last Light

Why is there something rather than nothing?
G.W. Liebniz 1646 – 1716

Wherever we are,
the world pads along,
rambunctious puppy,
fetching trees and rocks and cars and sky,
laying them at our feet.

Good dog. Big bones!

People we love
may or may not be present.
People who wouldn't mind hurting us
add an element of suspense.

For consolation,
nature opens her art show
in every direction.

The sheer arbitrariness is stunning.
Why doesn't the energy
imprisoned in matter
escape like the steam
from a screaming kettle?

What have we done
to deserve this world?

And when the time comes
to leave it, as that damn dog
runs away, why
should there be nothing,
rather than the something
whose leash
we are bound
to release?

Stanzas

1.

Single tree on fire
cold under mottled sky as
starling thumps window

2.

Peaks buried in snow
black mud where tide falls away
soon the fog will rise

3.

Fly inert on sill
a breath tumbles him over
the wind on my face

The Carapace

I'm most encumbered where I go alone
The Eye Divine provides no place to hide
I search for One, find the Many are at home

I long for spirit but am left with bone
The carapace abandoned by the tide
I'm most encumbered where I go alone

This whiskey bears the taste of bitter loam
God's Holy Vessel asks me for a ride
I search for One, find the Many are at home

Her eyes obscured, she whispers on the phone
Her baby cries, she tells the sitter lies
I'm most encumbered where I go alone

The road tilts hard, she strokes so slow
Calligraphy of longing on my thighs
I search for One, find the Many are at home

She descends on me in flaming snow
I come alive that instant when I die
Now disencumbered and not alone
I end in One, where the Many are at home

Stub Born

When fingers fumble,
all things fall
butter side down.
If the cheese is removed
from the teeming fridge,
milk spurts to the floor.
Mud on the slope
drops butt to the ground,
best pants, of course.
Box precariously
placed on a shelf
waits, as if innocent,
in plain brown flanks,
to pierce with sharp corner
unsuspecting bald head.
The way is through,
even through
the passionate cursing,
the hopping while clutching
lanced big toe,
the fervent bewailing
of what definitely is,
useless yet inevitable.

Vibrating with dismay,
he flops backward and screams
in the aisle of the grocery store
for a two dollar toy
almost broken already
in its clear plastic sheath.
His head grinds in the grime
left by thousands of shoes.
Pumping tears reflect

yellow fluorescence.
His mother, Hera, her face
far above, wreathed
in clouds of wisdom,
stares at her shopping list
and waits.

Pathetic Fallacy

Water's face broken
into scales of a fish.

Clouds descend,
wanting to rain.

Now they are.

Nothing is missing.
The Fall is in my mind,
Resurrection happens -
all the time.

When I realize this, happiness;
when I don't, despair,
or indifference,
as sun breaks through
pale water near the island.

Nothing, nothing,
and more nothing,
Sunyata, the Void, rampant
on a field of nothing,
emerging into

Catch

Without pole or line
or hook, just bait,
I stand on the verge,
hoping you'll breach
and land in my arms.

Across the harbor,
trees fall in the wind.
The owl flies backward.
Pine needles dart
into my face.

Then the light drowns:
you rise from abyss,
reveal your flukes:
The water is whiskey
and I want to dance.

Your kiss will be
the death of me, I know.
Moon, unzipped by clouds,
winks and bolts. I await
your pleasure.

Meditation 101

Before me, darkness suffused in damask
holds spasm of blobs, sultry ingots, tremble
of emblems overlaid on fields of sinuous form,
tinted in murky fluid, set adrift to wander,
at random, across the obscure ellipse of vision.

Within this sack of protoplasts hanging
from my crown, motilities scoot, plod, unfurl,
abate, surge through inner seas, wobble off plumb,
ooze like paramecia, thrust into fissures
of cortical substance, gore secluded entrails,
lure me to follow the itch,
the pang, the excitation.

Tick of baseboard heater calibrates
abrasive clamor of engines combusting
grease liquefied from saurians,
as my tendons bend and softly snap
with each muscular adjustment.
Dogs yelp in distant yards,
and labored respirations
hiss to clicks from the withering
of seasoned planks.

In my mouth, faint after-taste
of burnt spaghetti sauce,
along with residue of cigar,
smoked tongue probing crevices
for shards of ancient pasta.

Aroma of mold ascends from carpet,
with edge of Speed Stick and soap,
masking the molecules released

from my carcass, to float on scent
of daffodils unveiled, just now,
outside the open window.

Skeins of mentation, variously alluring,
arc-white from a welding torch,
braid themselves into memories
of dubious significance, burning
strands of grievance, random to-do,
and lubricious cords of desire
beguiling my attention
into reveries of ardor
improbably, yet devoutly,
to be consummated.

All these, and more, swirl in cotillion
revolving through this endless space
where I search in vain, with the ragged
rhythm of my breath, in gradually
ebbing desperation, for what
could possibly
be me.

Riddle

He yearns to clasp Her empty chest
but She cannot be held.

He needs to kiss Her sizzling lips
but She will not submit.

He would give his very marrow
to succumb between Her thighs

and pierce the Holy Sepulchre
but She has no body.

Who is She?

The Nerve

Footsteps boomed
down the basement stairs,
then a banging, ever louder,
on the flimsy door.
For years, I woke
when this dark presence
broke my sleep.
Until, one night,
enough.
I ran to the door
and threw it open.
The shadow, defied,
trembled,
took flight.

Leftovers

This is the mystic church
of the double A battery
wedged in a grate on the sidewalk,
of the cat vomit with white worms
on the living room couch,
of the sudden ache radiating
down the left arm.

Our relics are the dry leaves
scuttling on asphalt,
the shit in the tread of our shoes,
the soapy scum at the edge of the river.

Our saints are the meth addicts
with stigmata of scratchings
on the sacred vellum of skin,
the lifers trying to sleep
through the snores and screams
of their fellow inmates,
the residents of nursing homes
strapped into wheelchairs
and staring at devils.

Our prayers are the boredom
of shuffling in line,
the queasiness of sailing
on a heaving ship,
the anxiety just before
the biopsy results.

Our priests are the vacant and ignored,
engaged in the hallowed rites
of standing alone in playgrounds,
choking on tubes in I.C.U.s,
staring at the ground in bus shelters
at three in the morning.

We call with little confidence
upon you, O Lord,
in your infinite absence,
to wake up inside us,
despite our finite compassion,
and redeem it all.

Day Sleeper

Vast heaves of radiance
against the blue curtains,
set to a broken opus
of Toros and Jake Brakes
and Harleys, as I ride
the horse of sleep,
ducking under dark
matted branches,
jumping stone walls
to bare hillocks
of almost waking,
only to fall back
into broken ravines
of deep emerald dream.

Later, the room seems
the same except that the light
has drained from the windows.
The books and pens and clock
are still on the floor beside
the bed. Against the walls,
the shelves and desk wait
quietly. I know that
hours have passed
and everything has shed
molecules and decayed
ever so slightly in time's
abrasion but I can't see
the change.

I could have been stranded
in a Gobi wasteland
under a snorting moon,
or set to wander in a sea
of snow ablaze with sun,
or simply cut off from self
never to wake again,
but instead I'm here,
back in the room I left,
still breathing, mind
beginning to tick,
so I stand up, put on
pants and shirt and shoes
and walk through the door.

Workshop

Amidst the usual dichotomies
of a Wednesday night in December:
hidden/overt, silent/loud, absent/present.
If I pay attention, and even if I don't,
You look back wherever I look,
from this page, for instance
in the white spaces contained
within the "e"s and "o"s,
in the ink of the dots above
the "i"s and "j"s, in the letters,
in the spaces between the letters,
in the words themselves
and the clusters of thoughts
that rise with each word,
in the lengths of space between the lines,
in the wide white spaces of the margins,
in the fibers of this paper,
descendants of rags and trees,
in the air pulled in, pushed out of lungs,
in the light that falls upon this page,
in the emptiness that fills this room
until it leaks out through the cracks
around the windows and doors
between the boards of ceiling and floor,
rushing out to create the space
between the trees and the brush,
past raccoon, coyote, and deer,
accelerating out from this structure
in every direction
to saturate the atmosphere,
swim through the algae patterns
of the clustered stars,
moving forever yet falling,

gathering all the matter
that's ever been formed,
all the time ever extruded
from the tube of experience,
all swept up by Indra's net
and flung with a snap of the wrist
to fall back and be absorbed
as quietly as snow on a pond,
by this ordinary piece of paper
that calls upon Your gaze.

Accession

Minutes before,
you were strangling,
your life, and my wife's, wobbling.
Now blood spatters the ceiling.
The doctor, who has yet to speak,
crouches
between your mother's legs,
sewing.
Nurses swab
the walls and counters.

For someone who arrived
so explosively,
you are calm in my arms.
At the window, we watch
the gray sky
resting on the rooftops.
Then, as your mother sleeps
and relatives clamor
to be allowed your presence,
you look up at me
through blue eyes
solemnly wielding the gaze
of a king
returned from exile.

Harbinger

(to Theodore Roethke)

After a bellyful of winter,
I want to dance, so when you barge in,
propelled by a current of cherry blossoms,
I step on your shoes and ride your feet.
We spin in the hall, careen through
the living room, smash the wooden chairs,
slam against the wall until the ceiling cracks
and shingles fall from the roof like rain.
We blast through the doorway, splinter
the steps, stomp deep into the mossy grass,
leaving your footprints filling with water.
We knock down the tangle of blackberries,
snap the scrub oak like fishbones,
incite a flurry of forsythia blossoms.
Holding tight to your belly,
I press my ear to the silk web of your dress,
listen to the roars and gurglings and flood
of hot blood. As we twirl in the stink
of heaving mud flats, you bellow out
your song of vernal combustion
to the green veil falling
upon the cheekbones
of feverish trees.

Seized

You in pursuit,
as near as this man
bearing my name,
wearing my body,
moving fast in the dark.

You in the trees
lurching past, lit windows
that bounce, framing faces
illumined by page or screen,
while the moon hovers
and silvers a nimbus of cloud,
Mars riding shotgun
on its flank.

You, both shadow
and quarry, present
yet unaccounted-for
in this night transit
of Scorpio,
tracking me down
until I am halted
and held

like the Ark in the Tabernacle,
besieged by Babylonians,
dust trembling from its sides,

like the clavicle of Simon
the Canaanite
in a tarnished reliquary,

like a mantis, praying
in the hands
of an astonished child.

SECTION 4: THE DESERT

Postcard # 4

On a straight road,
the mind unrolls itself.
Left elbow propped on left knee,
I steer this rented Chevy Classic
with two left fingers and a thumb
at eighty miles an hour,
piercing with our cool beige bubble
the heat that shimmies up from tar.
Shreds of cream cling to bowl of sky
overturned upon a plate
of desert licked clean.

Prairie dogs pray at edge of lane,
upright, paws limp, gaze
fixed on flat horizon.

In the pinon, ravens wait
to ascend with the bodies
of the most devout.

Rancho De Los Brujos

The Hobart dish machine subsides
as sun smolders behind the cliffs.
Bats stutter from the arroyo;
voices swirl, entangle, dissipate
in the breeze drifting up from the Chama.

We run to the alfalfa field
below dark hulks of mesas,
fall entangled in the loam,
trace the drumming in our blood
back to its source.

Spill of sunset evaporates from sky.
Lights blaze among cottonwoods
where rustlers were hanged
and brujos prowled the shadows
in search of wayward children.

Meteors scratch our retinas,
one flares so hot it sizzles,
leaving a green streak
suspended, for a moment,
before it fades.

Our bodies tilt the world
until, no longer looking up,
we're looking down,
barely held from falling
into the Milky Way.

Through the night,
in the space between stars,
more stars appear,
then more between them,
until all the darkness burns.

Old World

Ravens step formally
among scattered shrubs
as we ascend the high plateau.
At the hotel, sprained wrist
gives way, styrofoam
cooler cracks. Along the rim,
heat sucks sweat off skin.
Edged by camcorders,
shoulder tattoos, and halter tops,
painted backdrop dissolves
into depth of Canyon, Grand
that fills the chatter
with silence.

We descend to Tuba City,
check in under smoking sky
as tribal police block the road.
Skateboarder in parking lot
says legal aid office burned,
one fatality. We remember
hand painted sign on highway,
drive back to desert
in blasts of red wind. Navajo
guide sprinkles holy water
to reveal
tracks of a velociraptor
who leapt,
skidded in mud,
and bestowed that gesture
for us, in stone, to trace.

Ritual

Sayulita, Mexico

A pelican rides the swells
just beyond the breakers.
His head tilts back
at an angle to his body,
lending him the shape of a hook,
his long beak, the pointed barb.
When fish come near, anchovies mostly,
but any denizen of the depth
who strays too close to surface,
he heaves his wings, long curves jointed
in the centers, lifts his weight,
ascends, and turns in an arc
away from the sun
in order to cast
no shadow.

Suspended, he peers below
and when he sees the shape or gesture
of his desire, he breaks his wings
back to his body,
into a flying W,
and hurtles down
in headlong abandon
to pierce with his beak
deep into the water.

Then he surfaces,
lifts his head,
gulps and swallows,
as the frigate birds,

eager scavengers,
flap close around him
to glean any morsel
of the body and blood.

Postcard # 7

Georgia O'Keefe said
she was told by God
that Pedernal would be hers
if she painted it enough.

Cerro Pedernal
is a ridge-topped mountain,
remnant of a volcano
that blew its ash
all the way to Kansas.

Once, I climbed the summit ridge
and awoke in night to find
that clouds had engulfed the world
except for my island of obsidian.

As the stars seared above,
lightning stabbed
downward in the mist below,
leaving me as the one
possessed.

Thought

Coyote waits
on scimitar of sand.

Inside this crown of bone,
scintilla leap synapses
fancy themselves
ethereal, abstract,
yet as body-bound
as belch or fart.

Clouds whisk the vacant sky.

Inside this crown of bone,
scenes from Golden Books
and finger-paints of loss
imbue the world
with desire
and abhorrence.

What moves behind the mesas
in the hollows of the night?

Inside this crown of bone,
thought, arises
self, arises
world, arises.

Sudden gash of star
above the chimney rock.

Inside this crown of bone,
the desert
ignites.

SECTION 5: THE CLINICAL

Back To The Top Of The Slide

She wants to be like all the rest
but I am the Flash, Green Lantern, Aquaman,
master of land and light and water.

Winter was an endless rain lost in a thicket
of devil's club. I'd come home from work
and stare, sedated, at the ghosts on TV,
longing for the time when I was alive.

Now spring fizzes in my blood, oh, what a relief it is,
and even though she watches like an owl,
I secrete the pill in a space between my molars
and spit it in the rhodies by the bus stop.

Going up now: notions, hardware, ladies' lingerie.
In a few days I begin to see, with crystalline precision:
ideas, projects, and compassion bubble in my skull,
putting colleagues in awe of my output's ferocity.

I buy: Dell laptops for my nieces, Craftsman table saws
for my brothers, dorm-sized refrigerators
and digital cameras for our daughters, a plasma TV
for the sainted woman who cleans our toilets,
and Shane company diamonds for the Mrs., although
the bling-bling doesn't help me much at home.

In hotel bars, this middle-aged reflection sweats
in the mirror between whiskeys, but transforms
into sparkling raconteur and wry Lothario,
able to make the most iron-clad saleswoman
laugh and appraise me, squirm on her seat,
think, why not?

A thirty-five thousand dollar R.V. blocks the light
in front of our house in Magnolia. I cleaned out
the savings accounts to buy it. She refuses to understand
that this desert-sand baby will be our retirement.

I find Jesus in the homeless, opening their eyes
with twenties and fifties, funding their journeys
through the stations of the cross. In fact,
this morning I blessed three gentlemen so hard
with cash that they held a ceremony under the viaduct,
making me a blood member of their tribe.

With Victor from the QFC, I'm planning
a combined book store, plant shop, and local cinema.
I'm managing an artist who does codeine rap.
I'm importing silk ties with anime characters.
I'm designing a series of men's colognes chosen
for days of the week with Wednesday
as a musky avocado.

After many nights without sleep, I'm a comet,
crashing into suns that go supernova,
while she's still back on earth, begging me
to see a doctor, go to an E.R., covering her ears,
cringing at concussions, while I spin free.

God speaks, as he has in the past: the lips
of an Appasionata cup mutter
that heaven is here, the earth has been transformed, we'll
never die. The spirit moves and pedestrians
sing hymns while you surf through their bodies
like that serial killer in the Denzel Washington movie,
only it's all good, as the young folk say, you're not Fallen,
you're my God and this is your doing, right now, as I greet
your incarnations with a hearty embrace, under clouds that

grow chubby faces and laugh
as they float over the Sound, to the Olympic peaks
that become Valkyries singing Wagner.

But eons pass and vision breaks down, thoughts too fast,
scattering fragments, cop gives me a look, horses whinny
in police stables at Discovery Park, flyer for the Lusty Lady
slowly floats, dances on currents up the glass slopes
of the new library, so beautiful, can't, say what?
I'm not, talking to, windows shatter, glass in my eyes,
searing, a demon, winged, scaled, huge, with breath
of Jersey chemicals, tries to grab me, too slow, chest
bare to April's chill, pants off, matches from pocket,
my beauty, astounds the masses, light the P.I., comics page
with the jumble, catches, spiral of smoke, demon laughs,
space clears around me for I am holy, anger rises,
shimmering bolts, beams of ions, slaughter, run,
sirens calling, no one dies now, even in this agony,
blue lights strobe, they all desire me, for I am the Reaper,
the Lover, the Prophet, the Chosen, the Lamb.

*

Somewhere a metal door slams,
headache throbs in layers of fog,
time and vision halted,
a fly suspended in maple sap,
limbs held tight and down,
tongue cut with thirst.

Someone sits beside me.
Her face is familiar.

Lazarus Rising

After a seminar
on teens who self-mutilate,
I leave the community center
and cross over a crook
of the Green River, its flow
as thick and lustrous
as a lobster's bile.

I ponder the impulse
to draw a razor
until red bulbs rise
from incision's kiss,
to press cigarette to palm
until smoke curls off
like wood shavings,
to etch the pain in flesh,
and flash the world
into a negative
that stops the scream.

My own teen depression,
invoked by the state of being
a creature of energy and impulse
trapped in the shabby sports coat
of a Catholic school boy,
found anodyne in Lucky Strikes,
Rolling Rocks, and fantasy.
I wouldn't harm my flesh,
surrounded as I was by peers
eager to provide me with injury.

Then the deaths arrived:
grandmother, uncle, father,

limbs breaking in the wind
until the redwood fell,
and I fled to college, away
from the miasma of grief
but found no relief.

Now, trying not to think,
I walk toward Pacific Highway
to catch a bus but
a persistent ridge
blunts every street.
I find myself traversing
a zone invisible
from the world of intention,
where barbed wire holds shards
of neighborhoods at bay
from blank realms of fabrication.
Houses lean on pressed dirt yards
bearing wrecks with hoods agape
revealing palates of rusted metal.
Garden gnomes smirk behind
chain link tangled in scrub oak.
Here, birds flit unfettered
with the freedom of the ignored
to pick their food from green decay,
calculating enemies and wind
with each rapid pulse.

No one is evident, although
I place a child's chalky face
in an upstairs window
from which awareness radiates,
as if what was beheld
were itself an eye:
a flecked iris,

an empty pupil,
a waiting presence.
This gaze endures
the strobe from a T.V.,
the flight of clouds,
the skitter of a rat,
as the ground bulges
with the pressure
from sorrow's
re-animated corpse
pushing and scrabbling
against the weight
that holds it
down.

Evaluation Time: 12:45 a.m.

She looked more like a student at Seattle Prep,
slightly ravaged from a weekend of partying,
than a homeless crack whore
but such was the case.

The prelude was hard to sort out
as it wasn't clear who called the cops
but when they arrived, she was outside
a Central Area house screaming
that they should shoot her.

In the E.R., the cocaine had worn off
and she was calm, oriented, coherent,
except that she told the social worker
she was God's Holy Harlot,
sent as a gift to men.

She laughed when I asked about that,
said it was a way to frame her situation.
She didn't mind her life
but wanted to go to college
and realized that she'd chosen
an unusual course of study.

In loco parentis,
I told her that no spiritual system,
East or West, would condone
an 18 year old selling her body
for crack. She laughed again
at my desire and dismay.

She refused the psych hospital,
as she really wasn't crazy
but agreed to go to detox
as a less restrictive option.

Years later, when I drive
on Aurora Avenue North
or Pacific Highway South,
I look for her, hope
I don't see her
standing at a bus stop
offering her blessings.

Driving: 3:30 a.m.

Late enough
that drunks expelled at closing time
have either fallen near their beds
or roasted themselves in wrecks.

Early enough
that the first commuters,
latte pullers with arms like Popeye's
and carpenters with job sites
two counties away, have not yet
opened their doors
to smell the dark's
clean sweat.

Night holds the globe containing
car and reach of headlights
as if about to lift and shake me
into a blizzard of stars.

I forget where I'm driving,
probably to some crisis
in a corner of the county
so remote
that inbreeding
is required.

I come to an outpost
on a precipice
where halogen lights
only irritate the gloom,

where med techs
in hair nets and blue scrubs
throw a football
in the ambulance bay
and go long.

Evaluation Time: 4:30 a.m.

On the gurney,
in constant motion,
she snaps her head up and down,
slaps her chest repeatedly,
speaks rapidly
to a host of beings, tracking
them with her eyes, interrupting
and gesturing, although
none of them are visible.

She gets up to shake hands,
white hair rising above her head
like a Q-tip, the hospital gown
revealing swells of flesh behind.

I know God's secrets
because the cops who brought me in
were the Father, Son, and Holy Ghost.

I'm here to escape
the evil spirits
trying to kill me at home.
The good ones told me
to call 911.

I ask if she wants
to be in the hospital.
She consults with the unseen,
her head swivelling to follow
their vigorous debate.

She finally asks,
her fingers spread
to indicate
the spirits of the air
in ranks around her:
Can they all come, too?

SECTION 6: THE MAN

.

Sam The Man, His Toe Nails Be

yellow and long and horny, just like he,
and his arms are black with grime,
and his teeth are falling from his head,
and when the people pass him by,
he calls out, "Arms for the poor?"
as if begging for bazookas,
or prosthetics,
but he doesn't get much
because he doesn't seem humble
and he doesn't God bless
and he doesn't shoot the shit,
or hold up funny signs,
he just be Sam, old Sam, stinky Sam,
the one who's out
and about.

Sam The Man Dances Past Macy's

oh, yes, he dances, with his Gene
Kelly feet, a couple of malt liquors
and his spirits rise with the speed
that spirits enter his bloodstream,
until he's living in Paradise!
Everyone he meets is an angel,
kiss them, no, they flee. Let them
keep their illusion, because they're
just God pretending that they're
not God, that She's this attorney,
manicured and made-up, calculating
billable hours and tapping her heels,
wondering what to have for lunch.
Amazing, cries Sam The Man,
delighted by her intricate mask.
He tries to spin her in a tango
but She deftly avoids his embrace
and calls 911 on her cell.

Sam The Man absconds,
propels his body, lurching
like a broken toy along
the sidewalk, past gaping
mouths, paced by his own
reflection smeared across
the windows, plunges
into the street, cars
rearing up, braying.
He careens down the secret
spaces between buildings,
his heart a spider monkey
zapped in the lab,

his breath a piston
in a clogged cylinder.
Why, he cries, oh why,
would God call the cops?

Sam The Man Sits With Elbows

propped on knees, dew soaking
through the seat of his pants,
in the park beside the Public Market,
looking out to the Olympics,
whiskered by clouds, lording over
the gray-blue sweep of water
that's crossed by wakes of boats
likes gouges on a barroom table.

Tourists, bright smears on Sam's vision,
walk carefully past his fellow travellers
who panhandle, sell drugs,
answer back to their voices,
under the precise light
of this Sunday morning.
Sam holds his head in his hands,
wondering just what is inside
this skull, that as far as he could tell
contains a blank area,
roughly spherical, behind his eyes,
between his ears, with no apparent
back wall, a place where thoughts
arise, in words or pictures, linked
to the pressures of mood,
surfacing and disappearing
likes the mouths of fish
gasping for food,
all within this silent realm
that holds the real Sam,
beyond hospital records
or booking sheets,
his most personal space
yet somehow not his,

accessible yet mysterious,
very close yet galaxy far,
not dark exactly, yet not light,
not heavy, yet again not light.

But just as the emptiness
turns ever so slowly
to look back at him,
someone cackles nearby,
a bearded old fart in a tam o'shanter,
(Jesus, where do these people
come from and why do they live?)
and the impending encounter
inside his head slips away
so he is back to his usual,
cranky and confused, aware again
of the tiny bugs crawling
in his pubic hair, of his back
in flames where he fell on the curb
while drunk last night.
Kill me now, he asks,
but death doesn't come,
not yet.

Behind him, a little girl screams,
piercing his brain like a six inch drill.
An arm's length away,
a kite strikes the earth,
cross-piece digging into sod,
green dragon emblazoned
across its surface. The tail,
fashioned from knotted lengths

of plastic bread wrapper
bearing colored balloons,
flaps in Sam's face.

Sam The Man Dispenses

tears from a mechanism of pain,
chronic yet intermittent, grinding
directly behind his eyes,
as he sits on a bench in Occidental Park,
recalling the first blow: a sucker punch
delivered in the playground by a kid
named Aloysius, brief whistle in his ear,
rapid shift in vision to the right,
jarring Sam beyond the piles of dirty snow
and the brick of St. Theresa's parochial school
into a river flowing deep beneath the earth.

That first was followed by thumps
in alleys, bars, and logging camps,
in factory rest rooms, fields,
ditches, and holding cells,
delivered by fists and two-by-fours,
Louisville Sluggers, rebar, jack handles,
and even, going back to when
Sam was nineteen, a Christmas tree,
lights and all, that cousin Ray,
drunk on schnapps and enraged
by a lack of presents,
swung like a battle axe,
exploding ornaments on the walls,
catching Sam with the foot
of the metal tree-stand
clean in his temple
where he still bears a slot
deep enough to hold a dime.

Sam The Man Dreams

by God, does he dream,
visions of breasts descending
to spurt milk in his mouth,
dreams of sitting down
in a diner and eating his way
along the counter, coffee
to meatloaf to coleslaw to pie,
but never getting full so,
of course, wakes up hungry
in his designated doorway.

But what's this in the paper cup
he always leaves beside him
for anonymous donations?
A ten dollar bill, folded twice,
but for real, hallelujah,
so he takes it around the corner
to the park by the courthouse
and buys a little bag of crack,
smokes it in the hot glass pipe
provided by the dealer.

Sam burns his fingers
and his lips, doesn't really
feel all that good although
he's definitely
not hungry
now.

On A Bench By The Pergola

Sam The Man watches
stomachs bouncing by,
and wonders why breath
insists on returning
to his lungs, and why
the muscle in his chest
keeps squeezing and relaxing,
squeezing and relaxing,
a machine clacking away
in an empty warehouse,
and wonders why images
appear in his mind:

right now, an alleyway in Buffalo,
where Sam The Man walked
holding his father's hand
hanging from a sleeve stained
with the blood of pigs and cattle,
calloused fingers circling his own,
walking together through an arcade
of trash cans, that led to another
alley, and another after that,
below a flapping scrap of light,
crossed by cat-gray clouds
with not even nothing
beyond them.

God Lives Inside Sam The Man

peeks shyly through his eyes,
takes in the various itches and pangs
and pains, hears the constant tone
of traffic, smells the aroma of shit
that never seems to leave Sam the Man,
even when he takes a shower
at the Day Center and changes his clothes.
For some reason, God really wants
that smell of shit and constructed
Sam the Man, Sam thought,
in order to get it, the full bore blast,
although maybe God also has
a mission for Sam, to save
a woman screaming in an alley,
or fall on an exploding backpack.
Sam waits, but the big chance
never comes, and that's just the way
God wants it, apparently.

Sam The Man, He's Dead, No

just sleeping but smells
like he's dead, that ripe,
and his head rests on a rough edge
of concrete, yes, in a doorway,
always in a doorway, as he dreams
of flying, keeping himself
aloft over fields as green
as pool table felt, by force of will,
although if he doubts, he falls, so
he's afraid he'll crash and end up
where he is right now, waking
in a puddle of his own urine
with hail bouncing inches away,
the worst possible place to be,
yet stuffed full of God, he thinks,
stuffed as full as a fifth of rye,
its seal unbroken,
stuffed like a Christmas turkey,
just arriving at the plate,
stuffed like a rich man's wallet,
dropped right beside him.

From South Of Downtown, Sam

The Man hears a *hough*,
a bark from deep in the chest
of a mastiff who's been waiting
forever behind a chain link fence
for the intruder
who has come at last.
A fist of wind
shatters the windows
of the building across the street.
Their clothes on fire, people
tumble up Fourth Avenue
like harvest leaves,
mourners wailing
at their own cremations.
Light expands, blinding,
right through Sam's closed eyes.
He stands up and drops his pants,
using this singular opportunity,
at the fall of time, to get it on
with the flowering sun.

Sam The Man Knows The Streets

and alleys, yes, he does, and slinks
his way through them, avoiding
the crack dealers, always edgy,
unless he's buying, but believing
he's blessed because everyone knows
he has no money, has never tapped
into the system, man, the system,
and his clothes are too foul
for anyone to covet, so Sam thinks
that he's as safe and free
as a man with nothing can be,
as long as he holds his temper,
but sometimes the rage rises
and Sam gets pissed off, having
nothing and all, so he barks loudly,
to himself mostly, but also,
on a Tuesday evening in September,
at three feral youths who take offense
and kick the nearly living shit from him,
only stopping when the odors inherent
in Sam's stained fabrics repel them.
So they depart, cursing and mocking,
while, in fetal position, Sam The Man
watches bursts of pain
revolve around his head
looking for all the world
like little quacking ducks.

Sam The Man Sleeps And Dreams

wakes and walks, finds food
in the kitchen behind the church,
relieves himself in the alley,
looks out through his eyes
and flinches
because the world
keeps thrusting itself
into his face,
every moment a jack,
sprung from its box,
bobbing on a coil.

Sam the Man Will Sometimes

chat with the boys and girls
from the shelter's outreach team
who look a little older than the docs
at Harborview, but not by much.
They offer him a cigarette
by way of introduction while they,
with calculated ease, shoot the shit,
talk about the weather, drizzle,
where he's from, Buffalo,
what he uses for a bed roll,
nothing? That's hard-core,
before bringing it round
to the corral, by suggesting
Sam could sleep in the shelter,
gets meds from the nurse, eat
after prayer in the mission,
a niche in purgatory to Sam
who ain't got much,
that's well known,
but holds on hard
to his last prerogative:
the right to yell "Fuck you!"
and he exercises that right,
but not before he secures
a second cigarette.

Sam The Man Can't Remember

his last fuck
and thinks that's a shame
because, resting in a doorway
with his hands in his pants,
he wants to recall each probe and thrust,
maybe in a heap of trash last winter
when the creature adjacent
lusted for warmth?

Memory doesn't hold much,
only friction and release,
but then brings up sweet Esther,
who'd suck him off for his day's take,
then leave to get high, returning
before dawn when the johns were inert,
the dealers absconded.
She'd climb in the nest he'd built
under a pier, wipe the cum
from her face and nestle close,
the two of them enfolded
in an electric blanket, whose plug
dangled above the Sound.
There she'd tell him tales
of the Great Bazaar on Seattle's streets
as the last stars screwed their way
down to the Olympics

until the Seafair weekend
when the ships were in
and she made so much money
and smoked so much crack
that she ended up
fellating the void

while a fireman pumped
on her rib cage.

Now, without her, he sits
in his doorway, unable
to get hard, watching
the beautiful women
who pass him by, knowing
he'll never have one
even though
he wants them all.

Sam The Man Twirls In The Street

Sufi dancer under trolley wires,
dimly hears honking and brakes,
high on something that he smoked,
now karate-kicking cars, blocking the buses
so the cops come and point their tasers,
force him back to the sidewalk
where, guess what? He doesn't make sense,
talks about Plutonians and bankers
stealing his bonds and the Great Goddess
who falls upon him at the midnight hour
so the cops call AMR and they take
his blood pressure, ask a few questions,
put on latex gloves to look for I.D.
but he ain't got any, long gone,
washed away in the flood
that Noah built the ark for.

He eventually remembers
that he's Sam The Man and shares
that fact with the triage nurse
at Harborview where he's put in restraints
for taking a swing at a med tech
who dares to say hi to him,
then he's medically cleared
by an intern who looks about twelve,
mouth-breathing when she leans close
to employ the stethoscope,
before sending him for psych eval
where he eats crackers and drinks sodas,
gets some sleep because
no one is exactly anxious to talk
with Sam The Man who looks scary
and smells worse but he's come down

and is no more crazy than usual,
wouldn't mind a warm bed
and a regular check but doesn't
want detox or the looney bin
so they wonder, what
would be the point?
Nothing to be done
but let him go free, body
and spirit, out to the streets,
to wander.

Sometimes God Sends Messages

to Sam The Man: the drip in a drainpipe,
the stare of a seagull, an old man exploring
his ear with a pen, the music pulsing
from a trembling car, and the light,
in every f-stop and shutter speed,
from the gray of a Seattle morning
to the visual caterwauling
when the sun barges in.

A Goddess in a yellow dress
approaches, Her body moving
like birthday balloons.
A definite signal.

Sam usually notices when God speaks
but often isn't sure what He's saying. Probably
the usual: I am who am. Don't worry, be happy.
Love your neighbor. Stay off the crack.
God talks to Sam like he's a moron
but Sam doesn't mind, figuring he's more
than earned God's skepticism.

This morning, each person on First Avenue
is a syllable in God's monologue, a note
in His song, until Sam gets into the rhythm
and slaps out a beat on his thighs as he walks,
noticing the various incarnations passing by:

a woman – a man – a man,
a woman – a man,
a man – man – man,
– woman.

Sam The Man's Name

pops up in the morning draw so
it's his turn to make the world.
From a doorway on Marion where
a trophy shop has gone out of business,
providing a throne of steps,
he creates with abandon.
Trucks spew particles in veils of soot,
suits and dresses strain against the grade,
pigeons calculate vectors of looming feet,
clouds hustle above like Medic 1
responding to a freeway fire.
Sam begets all this
in pulsing waves from his brow,
forms a flake of mascara on curve of cheek,
a stain that meanders down a portico,
the otter's breath wafting up from the piers.
Keeping time with his left hand, he leans
over to adjust his greasy underwear,
and feels a chill, so brings slowly,
around the façade and into the alcove,
light, hot from his nearest star.

A Fly, Plump As A Donut

makes sweeping arcs
above the bowed pates.
Sam The Man returns to himself,
wonders where the fuck he is,
until the wheeze of the organ,
braying like a whipped mule,
reminds him: mission, sermon,
the price of a meal, so he must
have been hungry although now
he's just a floating head in a lab,
his body a vague pressure below.

His mind twists through tunnels
while the hymns drone on.
He wonders if God is near
but a cloud, dense and sodden,
keeps him from any contact
with the divine. Sam wonders
what the point is of being poor
and scaly, as full of stink
as a closet of fish
if he can't have God?

The minister parts his hands
and reminds the men
of their grievous sins.
Metal chairs screech in response
as they stand to sing.
Sam gives the finger to the pastor
but the holy eyes are closed.

When the pain kicks in,
Sam bends over and moans,
fire in the web of nerves
giving shape to his body.
Sam leans into it, discovering,
he thinks, what God feels.

Sequestered In His Cell

because he doesn't play well with others,
Sam The Man attends to the chorale of county jail:
undulation of voices punctuated by clash of metal,
the occasional shriek, pounding of basketballs
on the balcony where high walls and barbed wire
prevent dribblers from dunking themselves
into the hoop of sky outside.
Sam is on a hunger strike, not for any
particular cause but because the food
looks slimy and alive. No one seems to care
although it's marked down on a clip board
each time he returns his tray untouched.
He was arrested for sleeping, sleeping at noon
in Courthouse Park where he'd been trespassed
and warned not to return. When the cops woke him,
he was in no mood to take shit but gave it so
of course they dragged him in. After five days,
fasting in limbo, he feels crystal clear,
pure awareness in a fierce body, honed to bone,
waves of pure bliss pouring through him until
he feels a call to remove his orange jump suit
and stuff it in the toilet, flushing repeatedly
and flooding the cell. Then he stands naked on his cot,
born again of water and the spirit as the tide goes forth
to baptize every inmate and corrections officer
from the seventh floor on down to the street.
He waits, arms flung out, for the inevitable,
the metal door pulsing with energy, until
the extraction team, helmeted, padded,
high-booted, shouting incomprehensibly,
bursts in behind wide plastic shields
that slam him to the cot. They truss
his wrists and ankles and carry him,

writing, penis flapping like a pennant,
out to the common area where he's dropped
to the floor to wait while maintenance
unclogs the toilet and mops up the flow.
From the angle of Sam's tilted head,
7 Upper North, with two levels of cells
and a central command station, looks
as if it's foundering, sliding down
into the waters engulfing the city.

Sam The Man Is In Love

with Rachel who gives him free coffee
after she opens the shop
because the first cup is too strong to sell.

As she moves behind the counter,
Sam watches the veins in her hands,
the edge of belly peeking shyly
from under her blouse
(that makes him want to press
his cheek against the pale skin),
her slight limp when she
gets him some cream –
these rather odd elements
inflame him.

He doesn't know who she is
and she's not interested in him,
being careful to mention her boyfriend
when Sam stares too long,
but she does look him in the eye
and chat as if he's human. No power
in the realm could stop Sam,
trembling with caffeine,
from being smitten.

What does he see
when he looks into her eyes?

An idol, an empty mask,
a mirror, a flame.

The ache of frustration
could only be surpassed
by the pain of rejection.
So, in the name of Desire,
he will renounce his lust.
In the name of Spirit,
he will ignore her divinity.
But in the name of Chaos
and all that's Unholy inside him,
he has to admit that
he still wants her.

One Night, Mary, Mother Of God

appears to Sam The Man as he sleeps
on a grate above a duct that vents
a sleek monolith. Mary spreads herself out
like a poster, flat on a concrete slab.
Her smile plays across the conglomerate
in a way that creeps Sam out so
he's somewhat abrupt: *What do you want?*
Mary gives a laugh that turns into a snort.

Sam The Man, we have our eyes on you
and we like your style: the lurch, the fall,
the scramble to get up, the way you hassle
commuters and try to pet every dog,
the boil in your brain and the bugs
in your crotch. You're out here,
representing for us, all the time.

Sam presses into his eyelids
but when he looks again,
Mary shrugs her shoulders.
Her robe lifts and reveals
a perfect pedicure. Sam replies,
Hmm, by us you mean…?

Oh, you know, my Son and his Father,
my Husband, I think? Well, that's complicated,
but I just wanted to come down and let you know
we think you're doing a hell of a job.

The building around them glows a beatific blue
that defines the fog. Sam The Man rolls over
on the grate and pulls up his collar
against the sudden freeze.

Uh, thanks, says Sam The Man, *and don't*
get me wrong 'cause I appreciate the visit
and all, but if you don't mind,
I'm trying to get some sleep here.

Mary holds up her paper-doll hands.
Oh sure, I understand, no problem.
She rolls herself up like a shade
and vanishes with a *pop.*

Sam The Man, As Winter Arrives

does not envy, in fact, he admires
the bums who are ants to his grasshopper,
who've assembled the necessary
provisions for survival on the street,
using grocery carts for lack of mules,
piling them high with stuff,
both necessary and luxurious.
Sam himself does not feel the need
for such equipment, as mere survival
holds no interest for him. He wants
whatever the moment demands,
remembering from Bible school
the words of Jesus
about the lilies of the field
although life has taught Sam
in a variety of ways that Jesus,
given little credit for his humor,
must have been kidding.
Sam only knows how to sleep
when he's tired, rise
when he wakens, shiver
when he's cold, as he is right now,
wedged next to a dumpster
behind a spaghetti joint,
his mind slowing
to the deliberate
pace of the snow that floats
down and covers him lightly,
out of sight of the cops
who might force him
to a shelter
when he'd rather sit
and watch

the steam of his breath
ascend toward the bulb
that glows
just above the kitchen door.

Sam The Man Stares At His Hand,

daring it to move. He sits
in the middle of the sidewalk
outside Bartell Drugs, a precarious
position, in clear violation
of Seattle City Ordinance
but the Cisco Red wine
is doing its job as he meditates,
even through the rotten rush,
on the mystery of free will.

Nails jagged, knuckles
ulcerated and wet,
the hand dangles in front of him,
last leaf on a broken branch,
but will not move unless
the hollow place
inside his skull
gives the command.

Therein lies conversion,
the power that would allow him
to rise and walk, take a bus to detox,
delouse and stand under flowing waters,
drink burnt coffee in church basements,
whatever he needs to get clean,
but then what?

Moving cards in a blur,
the clouds cover and uncover
the sun. Now you see it, now you…

the fingers twitch.

Sam The Man Ascends

through a well of glacial water
under a circle of dim light
that undulates and expands
until he breaks its plane.
He opens his eyes
to a patch of black mold
in the center of a ceiling tile,
a steady beep beside his bed,
curtains on either side.
A television high on the wall
pulses color from its screen.
A great weight sits on his chest,
presses him down as he tries
to breathe carefully around it
but is met with a flash of pain.
He grips a metal rail and notices
first that his wrist is clean
and then that he doesn't itch
anywhere on his body,
as he recalls hands in gloves
turning him and washing him.
A strangled snore penetrates
from behind the curtain,
Sam tries another breath.
Up on the screen, an angel,
grinning in a purple leotard,
offers herself repeatedly
to Sam as she demonstrates
a device of curved tubing
that helps her do sit-ups.

Sam The Man Thought He'd Given Up

but, as he walks along the waterfront
on a morning that gleams like foil,
past the cruise ships headed to Alaska,
pains and pressures snaking through him,
he realizes that he hasn't nearly given up
as much as he thought, that he still has plenty
more to go. He sits on a large brown rock
on the beach at Myrtle Edwards Park,
above the grumble of water advancing
and retreating. Gulls eye him hungrily
as he throws clothes in a heap on the sand.
Under an indifferent glare, he removes
his legs, yanking them off, tossing them
out on the tide where a sea lion grabs one
and gnaws. Then Sam detaches his trunk
below the collarbone, shivering slightly
when his heart pulls away, spurting
from its vessels. He pushes at the duffel bag
of bones and organs so it flops to the water,
the gulls flapping in to peck the skin.
His head is hardest to remove
as he has trouble gaining leverage.
Eventually, his arms pop it off the neck
and jam it down on a point of rock.
Then the arms, joined across the shoulders,
hold hands to form a hoop that rolls,
bumping, down the bike path. His mouth
tries to blow away the flies. Nose melts,
followed by cheeks, chin, and eyes, liquid
flesh in rivulets that spread in a dark stain
across the rock face. Bits of brain bulge
from the sockets, and drift off like tufts
of insulation until his skull is reduced

to an echoing vault. An ant enters through
the nasal cavity and walks upside down,
dropping when the bone crumbles.
The powder left behind scatters and drifts
in eddies of smoke toward the grain towers.
A swarm of thoughts buzz like hornets,
but eventually leave to seek another host.
When he is only rock and air
and grass and water, awake
in the light, then Sam knows
that he's finally given up.

Through The Open

boxcar door, on his first trip west,
Sam The Man enjoys the movie,
featuring a jitterbug of earth curves,
wires snapping up to their poles
and down again, clouds shuttling
on backdrops of blue and gray.
At dusk Sam pushes his head out,
hair whipped by the side wind,
to watch the sun haul the twin diesels
toward the horizon soaked
in burgundy. He thrusts
his hips out the door, his piss
golden down the cars.

Dissolve to a night of jouncing stars
that Sam watches from his box seat,
wedged in a cardboard corner,
pelvis aching from the grind
of metal on metal below.
Occasional bullets of light
flash across the screen,
as he dreams, asleep or awake,
of high mountain corrals
holding unbroken horses,
sudden space in the leaf cover
when he fells a tree, maybe
pulling nets in Aleutian waters,
earning enough to build a cabin
in a glade guarded by nymphs.

He's young and strong,
with nothing behind him
but nothing above him,
the star of this movie.
What could possibly
go wrong?

PREVIOUS PUBLICATIONS

Homeopathic, Smoke: An Anthology of Smoke, 2009

Mass In B Minor, The Dupage Review, 2008

Nocturnal, published in Presence: The Journal Of International Spiritual Direction, as a Finalist for their International Spiritual Poetry Competition, 2007

On The Fulcrum: chosen for The Poetry Corners Exhibition, Bainbridge Island, WA 2008

Orison, published in Presence: The Journal Of International Spiritual Direction, as a Finalist for their International Spiritual Poetry Competition, 2006

Pater Noster, chosen for The Poetry Corners Exhibition, Bainbridge Island, WA 2009

Pathetic Fallacy, selected to be sung in The Last Poem On Earth: A Jazz Oratorio, and published in The Last Poem On Earth Chapbook.

Quite Contrary, selected for An Anthology Of Contemporary Love Poems, 2009, published by The Blue Fog Journal, the national literary magazine of the Nation Of Fiji.

Rancho De Los Brujos, kaleidoscope, 2008

Sam The Man Dispenses, and *God Sends Messages To Sam The Man*, published in Empty Shoes: An Anthology On The Hungry And The Homeless, Popcorn Press, 2009.

Spellbound, kaleidoscope, 2008

Stub Born, chosen for The Poetry Corners Exhibition, Bainbridge Island, WA 2007

Technique, Exhibitions, 2005

The Waning, finalist in a short poem competition sponsored by Binnacle and published in their collection of short poems 2008.

Yi-Han The Younger, Pontoon: An Anthology Of Washington State Poetry, 2006

My thanks to John Willson for his Poetry Workshop sponsored by the Bainbridge Island Parks and Recreation department. This book would not exist without the encouragement and close readings I received from John and the workshop participants on those Wednesday evenings. Thanks to Chris Peters for his technical expertise and support. And, as always, here's to my friends for being there, and to my family, Gail, Joe, and Matt, for being here.

For more information, go to
http://samrogers2000.blogspot.com/

Sam Rogers has a background in English Literature, Film Studies, Bus Driving, and Clinical Social Work. He works in Mental Health and lives with his family near Puget Sound.

9 780984 718306